Making
Ribbon Leis
and Other Gifts of Aloha

Coryn Tanaka
and May Masaki

Basic Bow, Money Rose, and Fairy by
Lisa Kaneshiro of Flora-Dec Sales Inc.

THE BESS PRESS

3565 Harding Ave. Honolulu, Hawai‘i 96816
808/ 734-7159   www.besspress.com

Design: Carol Colbath

Photography: Reginald Yee, Ace Portrait Studio

Library of Congress Cataloging-in-Publication Data

Tanaka, Coryn.
  Making ribbon leis and other gifts of
aloha / Coryn Tanaka and May Masaki.
      p.   cm.
  Includes illustrations.
  ISBN 1-57306-138-7
  1. Leis - Hawaii. 2. Leis.
I. Masaki, May. II. Title.
SB449.5.L4.T36 2002   745.923-dc21

Printed in Korea

~ Contents ~

Acknowledgments

~ Special mahalos to ~

Carol Mito for getting my mom and me involved in making ribbon leis.

Vera Fong for helping us get our first class started at Kānewai Park, which we still have on Tuesday nights; to Pam Okihara for allowing us to use Kānewai Park; and to our students, who have become our very close friends over the years: Sandra Lee, Hazel Yoshida, Kathryn Horikawa, Kimie Nakama, Carolyn Yokoyama, Kathleen Bates, Shizuko Umetsu, Caryl Tsutsui, Lucy and many more who have shared their time, views, criticisms, and ideas with us, and encouraged me to finish this book.

Devin Kohara, Barbara Tong, and Lei Momi Dela Pena from Mōʻiliʻili Community Center for working with us to offer additional classes at the center.

Sidney Hamada, Walter Jinbo, LiSa Kaneshiro, and the rest of the staff at Flora-Dec for allowing us to offer a class there, for allowing us be a part of their large family, and for their contributions to this book.

My friends and family at St. Louis Drive In: Wayne, Irene, Val, John, Dan, Kathleen, and the rest for their added support.

Our family: my dad, Edward Masaki, my husband, Randal Tanaka, and my sons Ron and Dustin Tanaka for all their help, encouragement, efforts, and muscles, while their mother and grandmother went bananas. But mostly to my mom for taking all that ribbing from me and for her great ideas (for humbug leis that turned out to be beautiful works of art).

Happy lei making!
Coryn Tanaka

How to Use This Book

This book is designed for use by both beginning and experienced ribbon lei makers.

The **Supplies** section describes the needles, ribbons, and accessories you will need to make the leis. To be sure you get the right supplies, take this book with you when you go to Flora-Dec. The clerks there are familiar with the ribbons and can answer questions you have about lei-making supplies.

The **Basic Steps** section includes step-by-step instructions (including photographs) explaining the techniques you will use to make the three types of leis included in this book. If you are a beginner, familiarize yourself with these techniques first; then, when you are making a particular lei, you can refer back to these instructions. TIP: Tie 2 or 3 12-inch lengths of ribbon to the top wire of the spiral binding and use them as bookmarks to make it easier to refer to sections you need to review.

Experienced lei-makers can skip the **Basic Steps** section and go directly to the individual lei instructions.

A two-sided grid for marking ribbons is provided at the end of the book. Just tear out the page and laminate it.

Leis made with the **plumeria stitch**: Beginners may want to start with leis made with the plumeria (gathering, or running) stitch (pages 14–19). This stitch is simpler than the pīkake stitch, and leis made with the plumeria stitch can be made more quickly than those made by cutting, shredding, pinching, and/or rolling.

Leis made with the **pīkake stitch**: The pīkake stitch requires more patience than the plumeria stitch, but with practice it is soon mastered and produces a variety of lifelike leis (pages 20–24).

Leis made from **cut pieces**: These leis (pages 25–35) require some preparation time, but the actual sewing goes quickly. These are the showiest leis, and most often mistaken for real flowers.

Pages 36–43 include step-by-step instructions for making a basic bow to attach to finished leis and two beautiful and creative gifts for birthdays, graduation, and other special occasions.

Supplies

All supplies can be found at Flora-Dec Sales, 373 N. Nimitz Highway, Honolulu. On the Neighbor Islands or outside Hawai'i, call local craft stores to locate ribbons by C & G and Schiff.

❶ Needles

Use beading needles with a large eye (found only at Flora-Dec), and the EZ needle pack with a #6 embroidery needle and #3 cotton darner.

- Use beading needles for leis made with nylon acetate, satin, or polyester chiffon ribbons. The small holes these needles make keep the leis from shifting or settling.

- Beading needles are very fragile. Do not put too much pressure on the needle when you are sewing or it will break and you will have to start all over again.
- Use #6 embroidery needles for leis made with satin acetate ribbons; the holes they make are big enough not to shred the thread, but small enough to keep the leis from settling.
- Use the #3 cotton darner for shredding ribbon.

❷ Thread

Use nylon beading thread; it is strong, but thin enough to fit through the eyes of the beading needles.

❸ Wooden Clothespin

The wooden clothespin is used for every lei in this book. It acts as a weight and helps the lei to spin. Plastic clothespins will not work because they are too light.

❹ Marking Pens

Use pens that will not bleed on the ribbons (test first on a small piece of ribbon). Rolling gel pens work best, but other nonbleeding pens are okay (pencils, too, as long as you can see the dots). We use Gel Roller Slim Marvy in black and white and assorted milky pastel colors.

❺ Aoyama Tape

Aoyama tape is an all-purpose double-sided tape. Use it to join ribbons that have been cut by the factory (in the middle of the roll), to make leis requiring more than one roll of ribbon, or to make leis with different-colored ribbons. You can also use it to give leis more body or to fix missed stitches (see page 5).

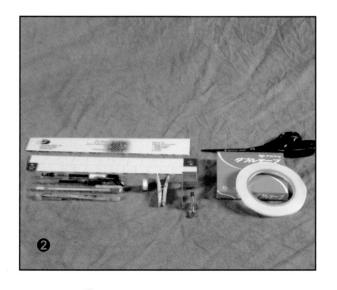

❷ Scissors

Use sharp scissors to avoid shredding the ribbon.

Measuring Tape

Use a measuring tape to measure your thread or to check the length of a lei in progress.

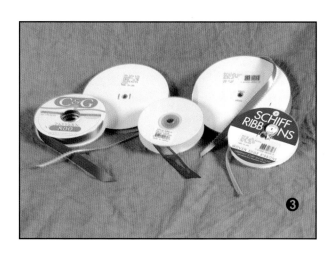

Measuring/Marking Grid

Use the grid (pages 43 and 44) to measure and mark your ribbons.

❷ Table Clamp

A table clamp (actually a "bouquet holder") is optional, but recommended. A table clamp acts as a "third hand" and will help you shred ribbon, open the petals of some leis, hold a ginger lei while you push it down tightly, and hold a ti leaf lei so you can twist it.

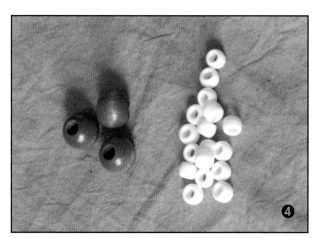

❸ Ribbons

Use only C & G, Schiff, and other brands of ribbons sold at Flora-Dec. If you use other brands, the leis may not hold their shape.

❹ Beads

The Naupaka, Naupaka with Ginger, Stephanotis, and Ē Koa Seed Choker leis use either wooden or white pony beads.

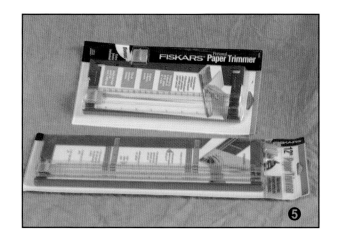

Optional but Useful

❺ The Fiskars personal paper cutter is useful for cutting ribbons for the Spring Haku, ʻŌhai Aliʻi, White Ginger, Naupaka, Naupaka with Ginger, and Micronesian Hibiscus Weave leis.

❻ An embroidery floss box or other container with small compartments is useful for sorting and storing cut pieces for the Spring Haku, ʻŌhai Aliʻi, White Ginger, Naupaka, Naupaka with Ginger, and Micronesian Hibiscus Weave leis.

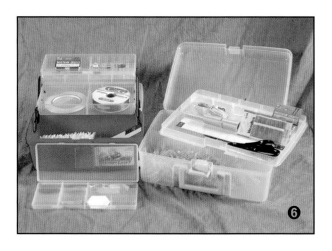

Basic Steps

Threading

For each lei, you will need a 3-yard length of thread. Use a measuring tape or stick, or simply pull your thread 2 times, stretching your arms out fully each time.

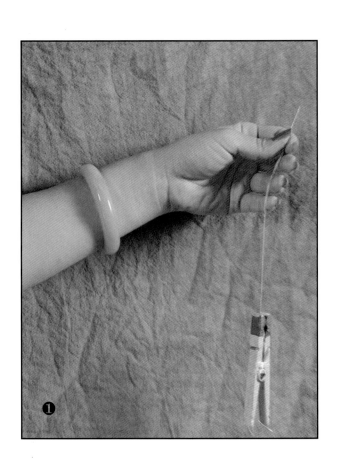

To help keep your thread from knotting, wax your thread (with beeswax or candle wax) before or after threading. DO NOT use a threader to thread your beading needle; it will fracture the eye and shred your thread.

Thread your needle, double your thread, and tie a knot 3 or 4 inches from the end.

Open your wooden clothespin and slide the knot of your thread all the way back to the spring. Close the clothespin and wrap the thread around the clothespin over the spring.

❶ If you wind the thread too far back of the spring, the thread will roll off the back of the clothespin. If you wrap it too close to the front, you will not be able to open the clothespin. Secure the thread between the tips of the clothespin, leaving about a 5-in. length of thread (from the needle to the clothespin). Placing florist's tape over the inside tips of the clothespin helps prevent the thread from slipping out or shredding.

Make sure your clothespin can turn freely. You can rest it on the table or on your lap while sewing, but when it's time to unwind more thread, you will have to lift it up and away from you and the table.

Marking

❷ Unroll the ribbon from the spool and mark with little dots at the intervals indicated in the instructions for each lei ($1/2$ in., 1 in., etc.). Use the marking grid on pages 43 and 44. Some leis call for marking down the center of the ribbon; others call for marking along the edge. If you're right-handed, place the spool of ribbon to your left and mark the upper edge of the ribbon; if you're left-handed, place the spool to your right and mark the lower edge.

When sewing two or three different ribbons at a time with different measurements, use different-colored pens to make the dots so you won't get confused.

After you've marked the ribbon, wind it back onto the spool.

Aoyama Tape

❸ To join two pieces of ribbon (of the same or a different color) place a piece of Aoyama tape across the end of one ribbon, peel off the backing, and attach the other ribbon. Make sure the spacing between the dots stays the same.

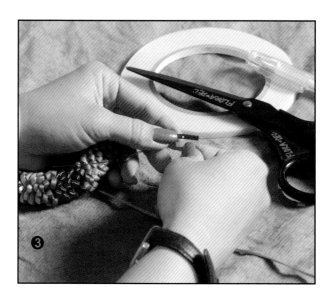

❹ To keep a lei from settling too much, place a small piece of tape over the marked dots at least every two to three yards. It will make your needles sticky, so you'll have to wipe them off occasionally.

To fix a lei if you've accidentally failed to sew through both ribbons when you've taken a stitch, take a small piece of Aoyama tape and place it between the two ribbons as close to the sewn edge as possible.

Stitching

You will use two basic stitches to make the leis: the plumeria (gathering) stitch and the pīkake (circular) stitch.

Plumeria (Gathering) Stitch

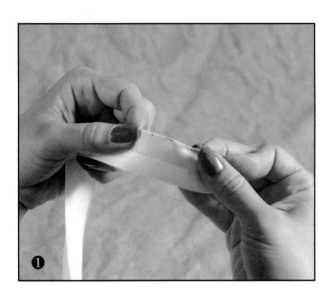

❶ A gathering stitch is a stitch that runs along one edge or down the center of the ribbon. Insert your needle in the ribbon at the first dot, either from underneath or from the top of the ribbon. Sew from dot to dot. It's okay to gather the ribbon as you sew, but flatten your work after every three or four stitches (an exception is the Cigar lei, which you should gather with each stitch). Keep the end of the ribbon close to the clothespin.

When you need more thread, unwind another 5 inches from the clothespin and continue stitching.

❷ Every 15 inches or so, you can form petals: With the clothespin, needle, and thread attached to the table clamp, face the clamp and push the ribbons toward the clothespin. Start at the end closest to the clothespin and pinch the ribbons between each stitch (or every other stitch, depending on the directions for a particular lei) and push toward the clothespin, twisting the ribbon in a circular motion around the thread. Be sure to twist in the same direction with each push. Follow the individual directions for each lei.

Pīkake (Circular) Stitch

❸ A pīkake stitch is a circular stitch in which the needle always enters the ribbon from underneath. Insert your needle at the first dot, from underneath the ribbon. Take your needle around the edge of the ribbon (the right edge if you're right-handed, the left edge if you're left-handed) and up through the next dot.

❹ When you make the stitch with your needle, rest your clothespin on the table. When you pull the thread, lift the needle, thread, and ribbon so that the clothespin dangles (don't ever hold the clothespin). Pull the thread toward you and the ribbon away from you, evenly and slowly.

❺ Pull the thread and ribbon until cones form. (Don't try to place the ribbon with your fingers.) The points of the cones should point upward.

- Pull your needle toward you and the thread outward evenly and slowly. This is not a race that you have to finish quickly. A quickly sewn lei is a messy lei.

- As the lei gets longer and your thread gets shorter, just release some thread from the pin and push your work down gently, a little at a time. (If your thread is too long, the ribbon and pin may not turn properly.)

- While pushing and sewing your lei, don't make it too tight or it will be flat; it should have nicely shaped cones, pointing upward.

❻ If one of your cones is facing down instead of up, release the stitch until you can slip your little finger or your ring finger between the thread and the ribbon. Give the ribbon a little push to turn it in the correct direction.

- Check and correct your work (if necessary) after each stitch. The ribbons have "memories," and the longer the mistake stays in the ribbon, the harder it will be to correct.

Tip: If you don't discover a mistake immediately and need to go back and correct it, don't cut your thread. Pull your thread taut and work the end of your needle through the completed stitches until you get to the mistake. Once the other stitches are off your needle, you can fix your mistake and continue.

Tip: When you put your work down, secure your needle in a paper napkin or a piece of cloth.

❸

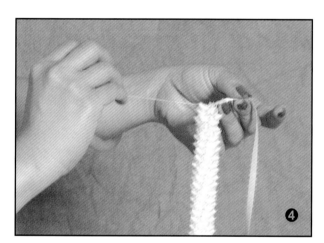
❹

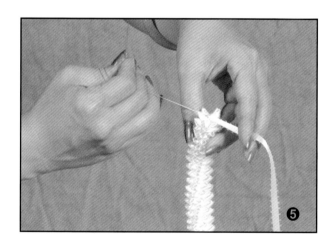
❺

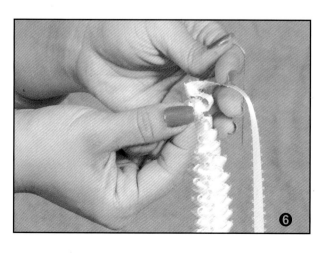
❻

Cutting

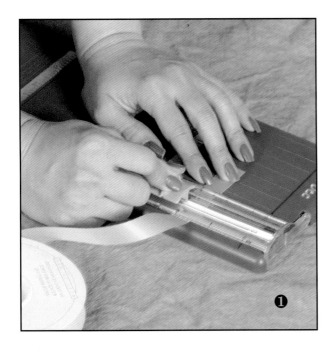

❶ The Spring Haku, Mele Mele ʻŌhai Aliʻi, ʻUlaʻula ʻŌhai Aliʻi, White Ginger, Naupaka, Naupaka with Ginger, and Micronesian Hibiscus Weave leis are made by cutting, shredding and sewing pieces of ribbon. Follow the instructions for each lei to cut the pieces. Use scissors or the Fiskars personal paper cutter (see page 5). Cut and shred all pieces before starting to sew the lei. Sort and store pieces in a box with compartments (see page 5).

❷ When instructed to clip the points off the corners of a piece of ribbon, cut as in photo 2.

To cut a 12-in. length of ribbon for shredding, mark ribbon at 2-in. intervals, fold back and forth five times, and cut off even with the last foldover.

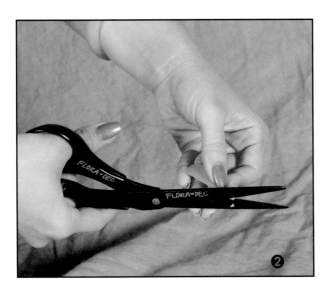

Shredding

Shredding is used in the Lehua Choker, Spring Haku, Mele Mele ʻŌhai Aliʻi, ʻUlaʻula ʻŌhai Aliʻi, White Ginger, Naupaka, and Naupaka with Ginger leis. Follow the directions in the instructions for those leis to cut and fold a length of ribbon.

If you're a beginner, it may be easier for you to prick and shred one edge of the ribbon at a time. Fold the ribbon in half lengthwise. Unfold. Hold the ribbon flat on the table with your left hand (or your right, if you're left-handed), and with your cotton darner, start in the upper right (or left, if you're left-handed) corner of the ribbon and prick the edge, starting about $1/8$ in. from the edge, to make a fringe. Continue moving downward until you've pricked an inch or two of ribbon.

❸ Starting at the top, grab the fringe with your right hand. Hold the ribbon flat on the table with your left hand. Pull straight out (not down), pulling the threads from the ribbon lengthwise.

Continue until you have shredded one edge of the ribbon according to the instructions for each lei (usually leaving $1/4$ in. of unshredded ribbon to the right of the fold). Turn the ribbon around and prick and shred the other edge until there is a $1/2$-in. strip of unshredded ribbon down the center.

❹ A faster way is to hold the ribbon in one hand, with the lengthwise fold toward your palm, and prick and shred both edges at the same time.

You can also shred ribbon using the table clamp (see Lehua Choker, page 17).

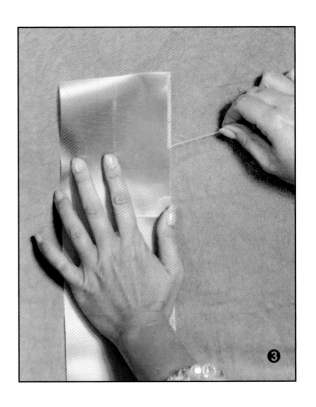

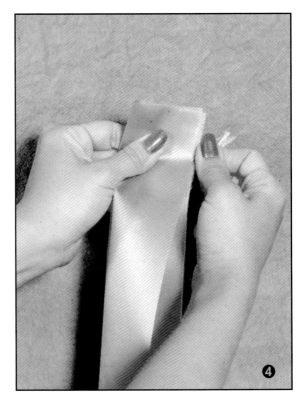

Pinching

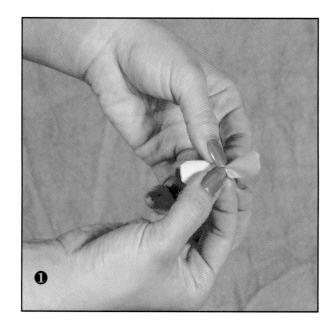

❶ In some leis, short lengths of ribbon are pinched and sewn into the lei. Hold the ribbon with the edges against your thumb and middle finger. With your forefinger, press the middle of the ribbon from underneath slightly while pinching, to form a W-shaped fold. Crease only the center of the ribbon, not all the way to the ends. Insert your needle from the side and sew through the folds to the other side.

Pinching and Folding

❷ To pinch and fold, make a pinch, then fold it in half. Insert your needle from the side and sew through the folds to the other side.

Rolling

❸ Rolls are used to make ginger leis. Roll (fold without creasing) the piece of ribbon into thirds and hold in the center. Insert your needle in the center, making sure to sew through both folded edges.

Hanging

All finished leis made with nylon acetate, satin, or polyester chiffon should be hung (vertically, not tied into a circle) with the clothespin at the bottom and the needle at the top. Do not cut anything. Hang the spool of ribbon over the hanger and place another clothespin over the end of the needle and thread.

The lei should hang for two or three days, to settle. If the lei settles more than you expected, add more stitches until it is the length you want. A good finished length for a lei is 38 to 42 inches.

If you are making a lei that you will need right away and won't have time to hang it so it can settle, place a small piece of Aoyama tape over the ribbon markings every two to three yards before you begin sewing.

Tying

❹ After the lei has settled and is the length you want, tie the ends together securely and attach a bow over the knot. (See pages 36 and 37 to make a simple bow.)

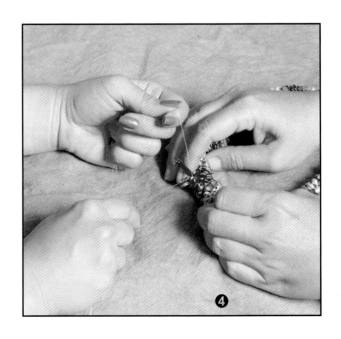

Chokers

Any lei can be shortened to form a choker. A good length for a finished choker-style lei is 27 to 28 inches. (Start with 3 yards of thread, in case you change your mind and decide to make a full-length lei.)

To make the ties, you'll need 1 yard black or brown grosgrain ribbon (³/₈ in. wide) and 2 16-mm or larger wooden beads or plastic kukui nuts.

Cut the ribbon in half to form 2 18-in. pieces.

❶ Fold one piece in half so that the folded piece is 9 inches long. Unfold and place a piece of Aoyama tape from the fold to one end. Remove the backing from the tape.

❷ Position the lei so that you have at least 5 inches of thread at each end. Place the thread at one end of the lei on the tape.

❸ Place another piece of tape over the length of the thread and peel off the backing.

❹ Now fold the other end of the ribbon over the tape and press hard along the length of the ribbon to remove air bubbles.

❺ Thread the ribbon through the bead until the bead is next to the lei, and tie a knot snugly against the bead.

❻ Repeat on the other side of the lei.

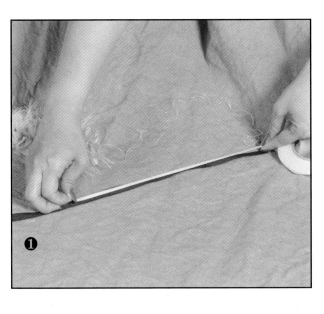

❶

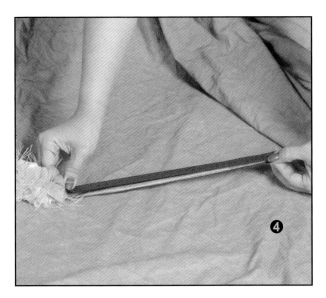

❷

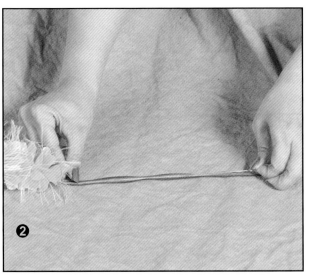

❸

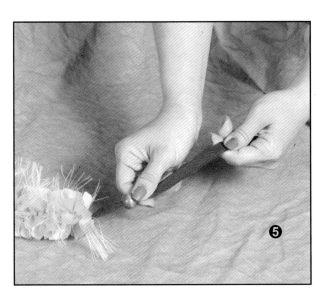

❹

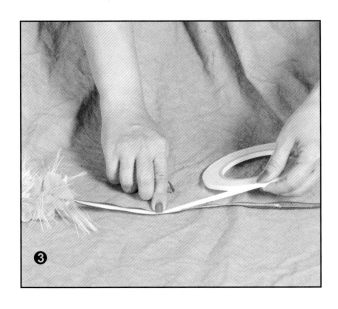

❺

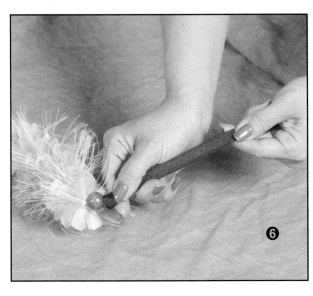

❻

Ali's Twist with Three Colors

- 1 roll (20 to 30 yards) $3/8$-in. picot (any color)
- 1 roll (20 to 30 yards) $1/4$-in. satin (any color)
- 1 roll (20 to 30 yards) $1/8$-in. single- or double-faced satin (any color)
- marking pen
- beading needle
- nylon beading thread
- wooden clothespin
- table clamp (optional)

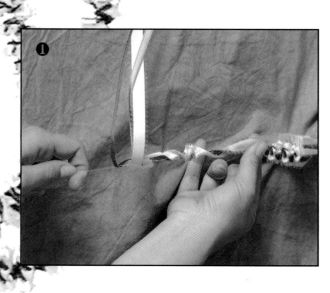

On the $1/8$-in. single- or double-faced satin, mark one edge at $1/2$-in. intervals (see page 5).

Place the three ribbons on top of each other, shiny side up, with the $3/8$-in. on the bottom, the $1/4$-in. in the middle, and the $1/8$-in. on top. Align the ribbons on the edge marked with the dots and sew a $1/2$-in. gathering stitch, dot to dot. Push the ends of the ribbons

down to the knot and keep the ribbons flat. Do not gather until you are ready to twist (see page 6).

❶ To twist, gather the ribbons all the way down to the clothespin, pushing from the end near the clothespin. Gently pinch all three ribbons and push down a little at a time. As you gather, make sure the folds sit on each other; the gathered ribbons will start to twist on their own (see page 6).

When the lei is the desired length, hang it (see page 11). If necessary, add more petals. Tie and add a bow made with the leftover ribbon.

This makes a nice graduation lei in school colors. Always use a white background (the wider, bottom ribbon). If the school colors include white, use white for the $1/8$-in. ribbon and the other school color for the $1/4$-in.

This lei can be made in only two colors; just omit the $1/8$-in. ribbon and mark the $1/4$-in. ribbon.

Lantern 'Ilima

- $^3/_{16}$-in. red picot (or feather-edge nylon acetate or polyester) ribbon, 20 to 30 yards OR $^1/_4$-in. red single- or double-faced satin, 20 to 30 yards
- $^1/_2$-in. yellow-gold single- or double-faced nylon acetate or satin ribbon
- marking pen
- beading needle
- nylon beading thread
- wooden clothespin
- table clamp

Mark the edge of the red ribbon at $^5/_{16}$-in. intervals (see page 5). Place the red ribbon on top of the yellow-gold ribbon. Align the ribbons on the edge marked with the dots. Sew a $^5/_{16}$-in. gathering stitch from dot to dot (see page 6). Be sure you have both ribbons together.

If you miss a ribbon, you can either start over or just take a small piece of Aoyama tape and place it as close to the sewn edge as possible (see page 5).

❶ To twist, face the table clamp and push the ribbons toward the clothespin (from the end near the clothespin) twisting them around the thread as you push (see page 6).

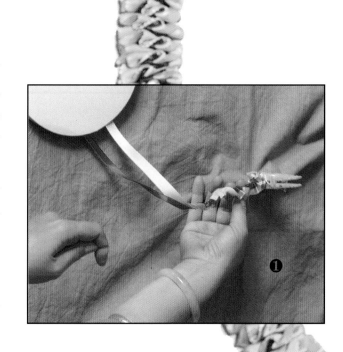

Open the petals. You should have at least five petals per flower. Continue pushing and twisting the ribbons around to form the flower. (The ribbons will get tangled; release the clothespin from the clamp and dangle it by the ribbons and they will untangle themselves.) Try not to push the flowers too close together. They should be at least a small finger's width apart. Continue doing this until the lei is finished.

This lei does not have to be hung. Tie and add a bow.

Royal 'Ilima

• 1 roll #3 ($^1/_2$-in., 50 yards) Valeria satin acetate ribbon

• 1 roll (25 to 30 yards) $^1/_2$-in. yellow-gold single- or double-faced satin acetate ribbon

• marking pen

• beading needle

• nylon beading thread

• wooden clothespin

• table clamp

Mark the edge of the Valeria ribbon at $^5/_{16}$-in. intervals (see page 5).

Secure the marked ribbon with the table clamp, about a yard from the end. Pull the loose end of the ribbon tight and prick and shred the unmarked edge (see photo on page 17). When shredding, try not to cut the thread; make it one long continuous shred. Keep shredding until you have a $^1/_8$-inch band on the marked edge. Release and start again. Shred 25 to 30 yards of ribbon.

Place the shredded ribbon on top of the yellow-gold ribbon, with the marked edge aligned with the edge of the yellow-gold ribbon, and sew a $^5/_{16}$-in. gathering stitch from dot to dot. Push the ends of the ribbons down toward the knot and keep the ribbons flat until you are ready to twist (see page 6).

❶ To twist, face the table clamp and push the ribbons toward the clothespin (from the end near the clothespin) twisting them around the thread as you push (see page 6). This lei requires a tight push.

When the lei is the desired length, hang it (see page 11). If necessary, add more petals. Tie and add a bow.

This lei makes a beautiful choker; you can also wrap it around another lei to change the style.

Lehua Choker

- #9 (1 1/4-in.) red, orange, white or yellow satin acetate, 10 yards
- 5/8-in. chiffon (Tri Mar or Jascotina), no wires, same color as acetate satin, 10 yards
- 2 16-mm wooden beads
- 3/8-in. any-color grosgrain ribbon, 1 yard
- beading needle
- nylon beading thread
- wooden clothespin
- marking pen
- table clamp

Mark the satin acetate ribbon down one edge at 1/4-in. intervals (see page 5).

❶ Secure the ribbon with the table clamp, about a yard from the end. Pull the loose end of the ribbon tight and prick and shred the unmarked edge. When shredding, try not to cut the thread; make it one long continuous shred. Keep shredding until you have a 1/4-in. band on the marked edge. Release and start again. Shred the entire length of ribbon.

Place the shredded ribbon on top of the chiffon ribbon, with the marked edge aligned with the edge of the chiffon ribbon, and sew a 1/4-in. gathering stitch from dot to dot. Push the ends of the ribbons down toward the knot and keep the ribbons flat (see page 6).

When you have used all the thread, let the clothespin spin freely while you push down from the knot end in a circular twisting motion (see page 6), making sure the chiffon is still under the satin acetate fringe.

Using the grosgrain ribbon and two 16-mm beads, follow the instructions on pages 12-13 to make the tie.

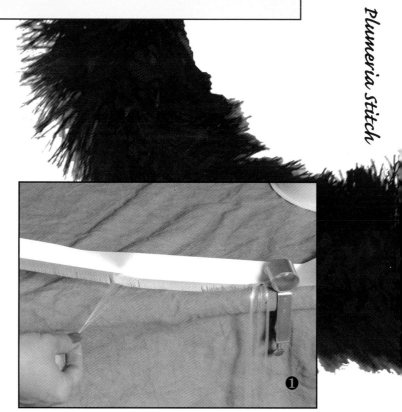

❶

Plumeria (Yellow or Pink)

- 1 roll (20 yards) $^7/_8$-in. white satin ribbon, single- or double-faced
- 1 roll (20 yards) $^1/_2$-in. lemon or pink satin ribbon, single- or double-faced
- marking pen
- beading needle
- nylon beading thread
- wooden clothespin
- table clamp

Mark the edge of the lemon or pink ribbon at $^1/_2$-in. intervals (see page 5). Place the marked ribbon on top of the white ribbon, with the marked edge aligned with one edge of the white ribbon. Sew a $^1/_2$-in. gathering stitch close to the edge. Be sure to sew through both ribbons. (See page 5 for tips on what to do if you accidentally fail to sew through one of the ribbons.)

Push the end of your work down toward the knot. Keep your work flat (see page 6).

Facing the clamp, gather your work toward the clothespin and start forming the flower. Pinch both ribbons between your fingers, between each stitch, and push your work toward the clothespin, forming one petal at a time (see page 6). When the ribbons get tangled, just release the clothespin from the clamp and dangle it by the ribbons and they will untangle themselves. Reattach the clothespin to the clamp and start again.

❶ While forming each flower, be sure that you have no more then 5 or 6 petals. Hold the thread taut with one hand and use the other hand to spin and open the petals. Each petal should be open, and you should be able to see the yellow or pink centers. Do not push the flowers too close together.

❶

❷ A finger's width and a half should be enough space. If you have more than six petals, your work is too tight. If you feel that some petals are too tight or too close, just drop the thread and use both hands to open or fix the flower.

❷

When the lei is the desired length, hang it (see page 11). If necessary, add more petals. Tie and add a bow.

Cigar

- 1 roll (40 to 50 yards) $^3/_{16}$-in. red picot (or feather-edge nylon acetate or polyester) ribbon
- 1 roll (40 to 50 yards) orange picot (or feather-edge nylon acetate or polyester) ribbon
- 1 roll (40 to 50 yards) $^3/_8$-in. brown picot (or feather-edge nylon acetate or polyester) ribbon
- marking pen
- beading needle
- nylon beading thread
- wooden clothespin

Mark the orange ribbon down the center with dots at 1-in. intervals (see page 5).

❶ Place the ribbons on top of each other in this order: top: orange ribbon, shiny side up; middle: brown ribbon, shiny side up; bottom: red ribbon, shiny side down. Center the brown ribbon between the orange and red so that an equal amount of brown ribbon shows on each side.

❷ Sew a 1-in. gathering stitch, pulling the ends of the ribbons down toward the knot and gathering as you stitch.

❸ As you gather the stitches, check the ribbon pattern every so often to make sure all the gathers spiral in the same direction. If you find that some gathers have gone the other way, just twist the lei and it should straighten out nicely.

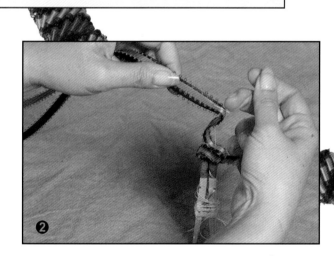

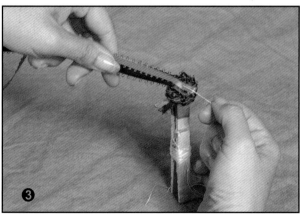

When the lei is the desired length, hang it (see page 11). If necessary, add more petals. Tie and add a bow.

This lei is also beautiful as a choker or hatband.

Stephanotis

- 2 rolls $^3/_{16}$-in. white picot or feather-edge ribbon
- 2 packages (about 120 beads total) 10-mm white pony beads
- marking pen
- #3 cotton darner from the EZ needle pack
- beading needle
- nylon beading thread
- Aoyama tape
- wooden clothespin

Mark the center of the ribbon at $1^1/_2$-in. intervals (see page 5).

❶ Thread the cotton darner needle with the first roll of ribbon and thread both packages of beads on (leave the ribbon on the spool, so the beads won't slide off). Push the beads toward the spool end of the ribbon. Unthread the ribbon from the needle and cut off the frayed end.

Thread the beading needle with the nylon beading thread and attach to the clothespin. Start at the first dot, sewing from underneath the ribbon, and work in a circular motion, inserting the needle from underneath each time (see page 6).

❷ Sew five petals, then slide one of the beads toward the petals and pass the beading needle through it, continuing to pull the bead toward the five petals. Continue from the next dot, sewing from underneath the ribbon, again forming five more petals and then adding one bead.

When you have almost used up the first roll of ribbon, connect the second roll with a small piece of Aoyama tape (see page 5). Mark the second roll and gently slide the beads to the end. Continue as above.

When the lei is the desired length, hang it (see page 11). If necessary, add more petals. Tie and add a bow.

This simple lei can be used with another lei by wrapping the two together.

Ē Koa Seed Choker

- ³/₁₆-in. brown picot or feather-edge ribbon (10 to 12 yards)
- 5 16-mm natural or nut-colored beads
- 2 16-mm beads of a different color
- ³/₈-inch any color grosgrain ribbon, 1 yard
- beading needle
- nylon beading thread
- Aoyama tape
- wooden clothespin

~21

pīkake stitch

Mark the center of the $^3/_{16}$-in. ribbon at 1-in. intervals (see page 5).

Thread ribbon through 5 nut-colored beads and slide them down to the spool end.

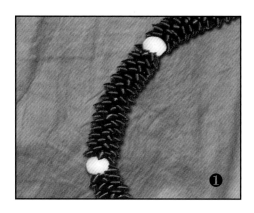

Starting at the first dot, sew from underneath the ribbon in a circular motion from dot to dot (see page 6). Every 150 stitches (about 4 inches of sewn lei) slide a bead toward your work and slide the needle through the bead.

❶ Continue sewing, adding a bead every 150 stitches (4 inches of sewn lei). The finished lei should have six equal segments. When you have reached the desired length, cut the thread, leaving about 5 inches.

Using the grosgrain ribbon and the two remaining 16-mm beads, follow the instructions on pages 12-13 to make the tie.

Pīkake with Rose

designed by Lois Inouye

- 1 roll (40 to 50 yards) $^3/_{16}$-in. eggshell picot (or feather-edge nylon acetate or polyester) ribbon (ribbons should not be too soft or the lei will not hold its shape)
- 1 roll (30 yards) $^1/_8$-in. shocking pink double-faced satin ribbon
- 1 roll (30 yards) $^1/_8$-in. emerald green double-faced satin ribbon
  - marking pen
  - beading needle
  - nylon beading thread
  - wooden clothespin

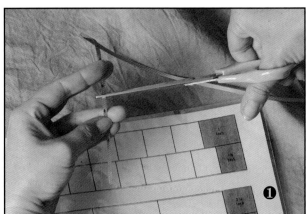

Mark the center of all three ribbons at 1-in. intervals (see page 5).

❶ Cut 2-yard lengths of eggshell ribbon, cutting between the dots. Cut 1-yard lengths of shocking pink ribbon, cutting between the dots. Cut $^1/_2$-yard lengths of emerald green ribbon, cutting between the dots. Note: Be sure to mark the ribbons before cutting.

Join the ribbons with Aoyama tape (see page 5), dot to dot. Join emerald green to eggshell, shocking pink to emerald green, emerald green to shocking pink, then repeat the pattern: eggshell, emerald green, shocking pink, emerald green, eggshell, and so on.

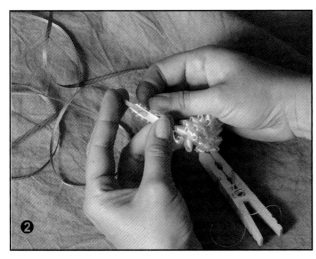

Starting at the first dot, sew the eggshell ribbon from dot to dot in a circular motion, starting from underneath the ribbon and continuing to insert the needle from underneath each time (see page 6).

When you reach the emerald green ribbon, use a plumeria stitch.

❷ Sew up through the first dot, down through the next, and pull to gather.

❸ Continue the plumeria stitch through the shocking pink and emerald green ribbons.

When you get to the eggshell, return to the pīkake stitch.

This lei should be hung for a couple of days after it is finished (see page 11). If necessary, add more petals. Tie and add a bow.

TIP: If you know you won't have time to hang this lei before wearing it, after every fifteen petals, place a small piece of Aoyama tape over your dot and sew through it. This should keep the lei from settling too much.

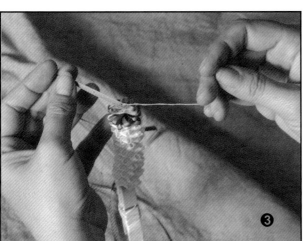

Pīkake Stitch and Plumeria Stitch

Peppermint Carnation

- 1 roll (40 to 50 yards) $3/16$-in. white picot (or feather-edge nylon acetate or polyester) ribbon
- 2 rolls (40 to 50 yards each) $1/8$-in. red picot (or feather edge nylon acetate or polyester) ribbon
- marking pen
- beading needle
- nylon beading thread
- wooden clothespin
- Aoyama tape

Mark the center of the white picot ribbon at 1-in. intervals. Then mark the center of the red picot ribbon at $1^{1}/_{2}$-in. intervals (see page 5).

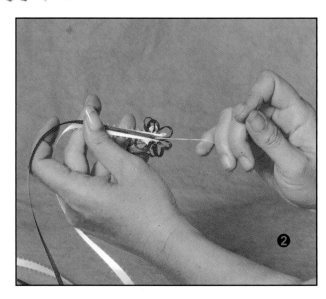

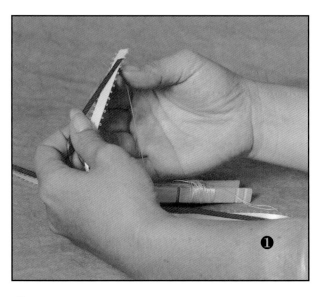

❶ Place the red ribbon on top of the white, with the first dots aligned. Starting from underneath the ribbons, push the needle upward through the first dots. Continue to sew from underneath (see page 6), aligning the dots.

❷ As you sew, pull both ribbons away from you and the needle toward you, evenly (see page 7). Be sure that the red loop is around the white loop. Let your clothespin spin freely.

When you have used up the first spool of red picot, join it to the next spool of red picot ribbon with a little bit of Aoyama tape (see page 5). Mark the ribbon and sew the same way. If you want the lei a little longer, join another roll of white picot to the first one.

When the lei is the desired length, hang it (see page 11). Tie and add a bow.

Spring Haku

- 1 roll EACH #3 ($1/2$-in.) satin acetate ribbon in these colors:
yellow-gold belle rose pink azalea fuchsia
orchid basil maize
- 1 roll #100 (4-in.) basil satin acetate ribbon
- 1 roll #40 (2 $1/2$-in.) white satin acetate ribbon
- 2 16-mm wooden beads
- $3/8$-in. any-color grosgrain ribbon, 1 yard
- #6 embroidery needle from the EZ pack needle set
- #3 cotton darner from the EZ pack needle set
- nylon beading thread
- wooden clothespin
- table clamp (optional)

Mark the centers of the $1/2$-in. ribbons (see page 5) at the following intervals:

2-in.: yellow-gold, belle, rose pink, azalea, fuchsia, orchid
1 $3/4$-in.: basil
1-in.: maize

Fold back and forth at the marks and cut on the folds. Clip the corners of each piece (see page 8).

Mark the centers of the 4-in. basil and the 2 $1/2$-in. white ribbons at 2-in. intervals. Fold back and forth five times on the marks and cut into 12-in. pieces.

Fold a 12-in. piece of basil ribbon in half lengthwise. With the folded side in the palm of your hand, shred the edges (see page 9) until you have a $1/2$-in. strip of ribbon down the center. Repeat with remaining basil pieces and with white pieces.

Cut the shredded basil ribbons at the marks into 2-in. pieces. Fold in half and cut into 1- x 4-in. pieces. Fold the 1-in. pieces in half and cut into $1/2$- x 4-in. pieces. Fold the $1/2$-in. pieces in half and cut into $1/4$- x 4-in. pieces. Do the same with the shredded white ribbon. (White pieces will be 2 $1/2$-in. long.)

When you are ready to begin sewing, lay the ribbon pieces out in sets: 12 basil, 6 belle, 4 yellow-gold, 2 maize, 1 white fringe, 1 basil fringe, 12 basil, 6 azalea, 4 rose pink, 2 maize, 1 white fringe, 1 green fringe, 12 basil, 6 fuchsia, 4 orchid, 2 maize, 1 white fringe, 1 green fringe.

❶ Starting with the basil, pinch and fold each piece in the center (see page 10) and sew. When you add the fringe, position the pieces so the basil fringe is perpendicular to the white fringe.

Using the grosgrain ribbon and two 16-mm beads, follow the instructions on pages 12–13 to make the tie.

Mele Mele (Double Yellow)
'Ōhai Ali'i

Cut Pieces

- 1 roll #3 ($1/2$-in., 50 yards) yellow-gold satin acetate ribbon
- 1 roll #3 ($1/2$-in., 50 yards) belle satin acetate ribbon
- 1 roll #100 (4-in.) yellow satin acetate ribbon
- marking pen
- #6 embroidery needle from the EZ pack needle set
- #3 cotton darner from the EZ pack needle set
- nylon beading thread
- wooden clothespin
- table clamp (optional)

Mark the center of all three ribbons at 2-in. intervals (see page 5). Fold the #3 yellow-gold and #3 belle back and forth at the marks and cut into 2-in. pieces. Clip the corners of each piece (see page 8).

❶ Starting at one end, fold the 4-in. yellow ribbon back and forth five times at the marks. Cut the ribbon off even with the last foldover. You'll have a 12-in. length of ribbon. Continue until you have used all the ribbon.

Fold one 12-in. ribbon in half lengthwise. With the folded side in the palm of your hand, shred the edges (see page 9) until you have a $1/2$-in. strip of ribbon down the center. Repeat with remaining 12-in. pieces.

❷ Cut on the 2-in. folds into six pieces. Cut the 2-in. pieces in half into 12 1- x 4-in. pieces, then again into 24 $1/2$- x 4-in. pieces.

When you are ready to begin sewing, put pieces of ribbon out in sets. One set includes 2 yellow-gold, 2 belle, 2 yellow-gold, and 1 yellow fringe.

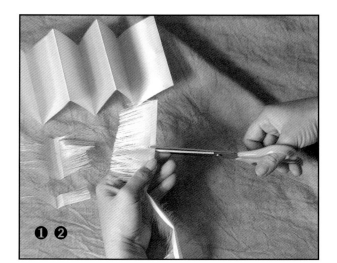

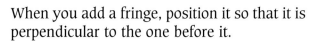

When you add a fringe, position it so that it is perpendicular to the one before it.

Push all of your ribbons down toward the clothespin. Repeat the same pattern with the remaining sets.

When the lei is the desired length, hang it (see page 11). If necessary, add more petals. Tie and add a bow.

I designed this lei and the 'Ula'ula 'Ōhai Ali'i and call them the "poor man's 'Ōhai Ali'i." They are a lot cheaper to make than many other 'Ōhai Ali'i. Both leis make beautiful chokers.

❸ Attach your needle, thread and clothespin to the table clamp. Starting with the yellow-gold, pinch each piece in the center (see page 10) and sew each piece.

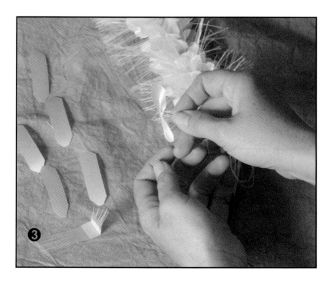

❹ When you add the fringe, open it up and sew a small gathering stitch in the center.

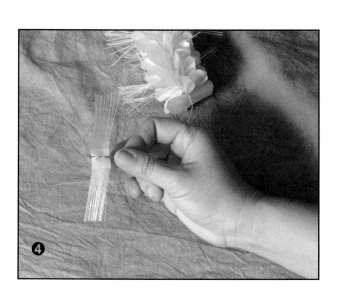

~27

Cut Pieces

'Ula'ula (Red) 'Ōhai Ali'i

- 1 roll #3 (1/2-in. 50 yards) yellow-gold satin acetate ribbon
- 1 roll #3 (1/2-in. 50 yards) belle satin acetate ribbon
- 1 roll #3 (1/2-in. 50 yards) red satin acetate ribbon
- 1 roll #100 (4-in.) red satin acetate ribbon
- marking pen
- #6 embroidery needle from the EZ pack needle set
- #3 cotton darner from the EZ pack needle set
- nylon beading thread
- wooden clothespin
- table clamp (optional)

Mark the center of the 1/2-in. yellow-gold and 1/2-in. belle at 1 1/2-in. intervals (see page 5). Fold the ribbon back and forth on the marks and cut into 1 1/2-in. pieces. Clip the corners of each piece (see page 8). Mark the center of the 1/2-in. red ribbon at 1-in. intervals. Fold, cut, and clip the ribbon as you did for the yellow-gold and belle.

Mark and cut the 4-inch red satin acetate at 2-in. intervals. Starting at one end, fold back and forth five times and cut at the last foldover. You'll have a 12-in. length of ribbon. Continue until you have used all the ribbon.

Fold one 12-in. ribbon in half lengthwise. With the folded side in the palm of your hand, shred the edges (see page 9) until you have a 1/2-in. strip of ribbon down the center. Repeat with remaining 12-in. pieces.

Cut on the 2-in. folds into six pieces. Cut the 2-in. pieces in half into 12 1- x 4-in. pieces, then again into 24 1/2- x 4-in. pieces. (See photo 1-2 on page 26.)

When you are ready to begin sewing, put pieces of ribbon out in sets. One set includes 2 yellow-gold, 2 belle, 2 yellow-gold, 2 belle with the red placed over each belle, and 1 red fringe.

Attach your needle, thread and clothespin to the table clamp. Starting with the yellow-gold, pinch each piece in the center (see page 10) and sew each piece.

❶ When you sew the belle with the red on top, pinch both ribbons together and sew the same way.

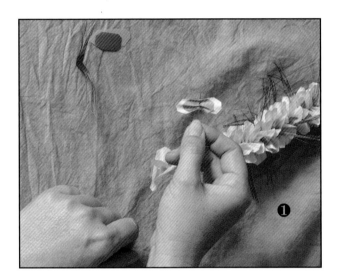

When you add the fringe, open it up and sew a small gathering stitch in the center. (See photo 4, page 27.) When you add a fringe, position it so that it is perpendicular to the one before it.

❷ Push all of your ribbons down toward the clothespin. Repeat the same pattern with the remaining sets.

When the lei is the desired length, hang it (see page 11). If necessary, add more petals. Tie and add a bow.

White Ginger

• 1 roll #5 ($^7/_8$-in., 100 yards) eggshell satin acetate

• 1 roll #9 ($1^1/_4$-in., 50 yards) yellow satin acetate, 25 yards

• marking pen

• #6 embroidery needle from the EZ pack needle set

• #3 cotton darner from the EZ pack needle set

• nylon beading thread

• wooden clothespin

• table clamp (optional)

Cut Pieces

Mark the centers of both ribbons at 2-in. intervals (see page 5). Fold the eggshell ribbon back and forth at the marks and cut into 2-in. pieces. Stack three pieces at a time on top of each other and fold in half. Do not crease them; just pinch the center. With the fold facing the palm of your hand, cut the ends to a point (see cut pieces in photo 1).

Starting at one end, fold the yellow ribbon back and forth five times at the dots and cut at the last foldover. You'll have a 12-in. length of ribbon. Continue until all the ribbon has been cut.

Fold one 12-in. ribbon in half lengthwise. With the folded side in the palm of your hand, shred the edges (see page 9) until you have a $^1/_2$-in. strip of ribbon down the center

Cut the shredded ribbon into 2-in. pieces (at the folds).

When you are ready to begin sewing, put pieces of ribbon out in sets. You will need 6 eggshell pieces and 1 yellow fringe to form one flower. Attach your needle and thread and clothespin to the table clamp. Starting with an eggshell piece, roll the piece into thirds lengthwise, with the shiny side facing out (see page 11). Do not crease it, just pinch the center. (You do not want the ends to have any creases.)

❶ Sew the centers of each piece, pushing your work down to the clamp.

❷ When you have sewn the 6 eggshell pieces, sew a very small gathering stitch (about three stitches) in the center strip of the yellow fringe.

Gently twist and push the fringe down toward the eggshell pieces and twist and then push all pieces toward the clothespin. This lei needs to be tight.

❸ Push in the center, close to the thread so you won't flatten the flowers.

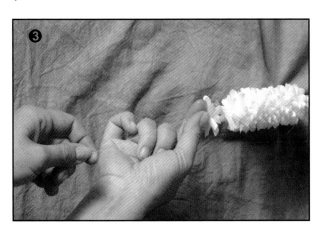

When the lei is the desired length, hang it (see page 11). If necessary, add more petals. Tie and add a bow.

This lei makes a beautiful choker.

Naupaka and Naupaka with Ginger

Cut Pieces

- #3 (1/2-in.) basil satin acetate ribbon, 25 yards
- #5 (7/8-in.) eggshell satin acetate ribbon, 25 yards
- #9 (1 1/4-in.) yellow satin acetate ribbon, 20 yards
- 6 or 7 packages 16-mm wooden bead (light or dark)
- #6 embroidery needle from the EZ needle pack
- marking pen
- nylon beading thread
- wooden clothespin
- table clamp

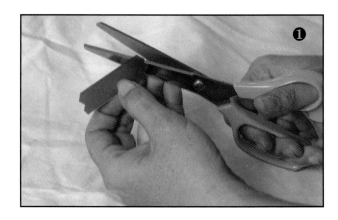

Mark the center of the 1/2-in. basil ribbon at 2 1/4-in. intervals (see page 5). Fold at the marks and cut on the folds into 2 1/4-in. pieces.

❶ Trim both ends of each piece into an uneven zigzag, freehand.

Mark the centers of both ribbons at 2-in. intervals (see page 5). Fold the eggshell ribbon back and forth at the marks and cut into 2-in. pieces. Stack three pieces at a time on top of each other and fold in half. Do not crease them; just pinch the center. With the fold facing the palm of your hand, cut the ends to a point (see pieces in photo 1 on page 31).

Starting at one end, fold the yellow ribbon back and forth at the dots five times and cut at the last foldover. You'll have a 12-in. length of ribbon. Continue until all the ribbon has been cut. With the folded side in the palm of your hand, shred the edges (see page 9) until you have a $^1/_2$-in. strip of ribbon down the center.

Cut the shredded ribbon into 2-in. pieces (at the folds).

When you are ready to begin sewing, put pieces of ribbon out in sets. A set includes 6 basil, 6 eggshell, 1 yellow fringe, 1 wooden bead, 1 yellow fringe, and 6 eggshell. Attach your needle, thread, and clothespin to the table clamp. Pinch each piece of basil in the center, then sew each piece (see page 10).

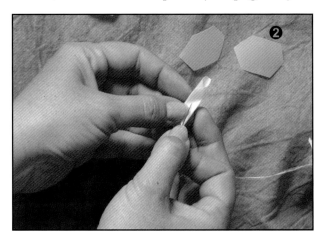

❷ To sew the eggshell pieces, roll each piece into thirds (see page 11), with the shiny side facing out. Do not crease; just hold the center and sew each piece of eggshell.

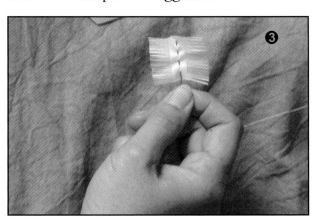

❸ Add the yellow fringe by sewing a very small gathering stitch (about three stitches) in the center strip of the yellow fringe.

Gently twist and push the fringe down toward the eggshell pieces and then twist and push all pieces toward the clothespin. This lei needs to be tight. Push in the center, close to the thread (see photo 3 on page 31) so you won't flatten the flowers.

Add a bead and continue with the yellow fringe and then the eggshell. Then start a new set. Be sure to end with 6 eggshell. If you are making a choker, end it with 6 basil.

When the lei is the desired length, hang it (see page 11). If necessary, add more petals. Tie and add a bow.

The Naupaka with Ginger, generally worn by women, works well as a choker-style lei or a hatband.

Naupaka

- 1 roll #3 ($^1/_2$-in., 50 yards) basil satin acetate ribbon
- 8 packages 16-mm wooden bead (light or dark)

Mark, cut, and sew the basil ribbon in the same way as you would for the Naupaka with Ginger, adding a bead after each 6 pieces of basil ribbon.

The Naupaka lei is generally worn by men.

Micronesian Hibiscus Weave

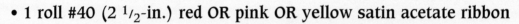

- 1 roll #40 (2 1/2-in.) red OR pink OR yellow satin acetate ribbon
- 1 roll #3 (1/2-in.) basil satin acetate ribbon
- marking pen
- #6 embroidery needle from the EZ pack needle set
- nylon beading thread
- Aoyama tape
- plastic twine (thinnest available)
- wooden clothespin
- table clamp

Cut Pieces

Mark the center of the red ribbon at 2-in. intervals (see page 5) and cut at the marks into 2-in. pieces.

❶ Cut the bottom edge of each piece in a wave pattern.

Mark the center of the basil ribbon at 1³/₄-in. intervals and cut at the marks into 1³/₄-in. pieces.

❷ On each piece of basil, place a piece of Aoyama tape from the center to the end.

❸ Remove the Aoyama tape backing and place the basil piece, tape side down, on the shiny side of a red piece, leaving about 1/4-in. or a little more extending out from the red.

❷

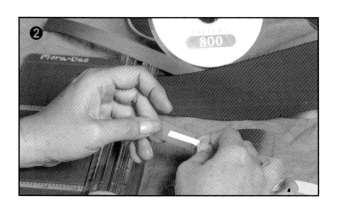

❸

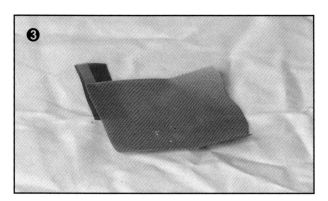

Fold a 5-yard length of twine in half and tie the ends in a knot about 4 inches from the fold. Anchor the loop with the table clamp.

❻ Slide rolled pieces, one at a time, to the knot in the twine. Twist the ends of twine around the piece, crossing over and under, where the basil and red meet. Pull the twine tight.

❹ Roll the red piece tightly until all the basil is rolled, including the $1/4$-in. tab that was hanging over the edge of the red. Continue with the other pieces until you have 140 to 145 rolled pieces.

❹

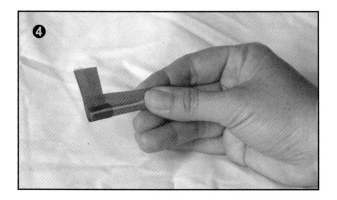

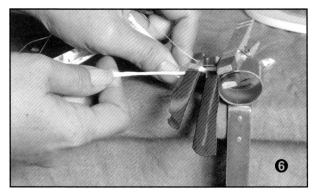

❻

❼ Continue to add pieces.

❺ With the embroidery needle and thread, string all the pieces, sewing through the basil.

❺

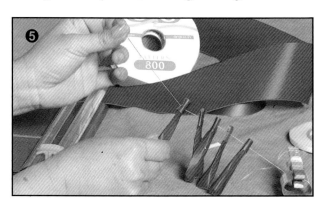

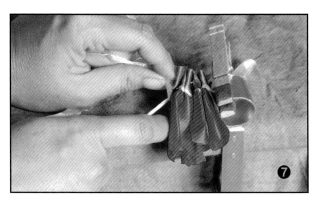

❼

When you have finished your lei, tie the ends together and pull your thread tight but not too tight. You want it to lie flat, not pucker.

Make a bow with the remaining twine. You may cut the thread and pull it out. I like to leave it in, to hold the pieces more securely.

Basic Bow

> • At least 1 yard of #3 ribbon (more if you use wider ribbon). Satin acetate ribbon (C&G 800 Satin) is an inexpensive, crisp, single-faced ribbon that is easy to work with. Chiffon ribbons add a soft, elegant look, but require more practice.
>
> • 1 chenille stem OR piece of curling ribbon OR florist wire to secure the bow when you are finished

If you are right-handed, your right hand is your "free hand" and your "holding hand" is your left hand. The reverse is true if you are left-handed.

❶ Hold the tail of the ribbon 1 to 2 inches from the end with the thumb and forefinger of your holding hand. The end should be pointing up and away from you. If you are using a single-faced ribbon, the "wrong" side should be facing you. You are establishing the "top" center of the bow, and you will build your bow from the top down.

❷ Using your free hand, twist the ribbon 180 degrees at the spot where the thumb and forefinger are holding the ribbon. The "right" side of the ribbon is now facing you on the "bottom," below your holding hand.

❸ Make a loop under and away from you. This loop should be half the diameter of the finished bow.

Hold the two loose ends together with the thumb and forefinger of your holding hand. Now the "wrong" side of the ribbon is facing you on the long tail above your holding hand. Using your free hand, twist the long tail 180 degrees at the spot between your thumb and

forefinger so that the "right" side of the ribbon is facing you.

❹ Form the next loop over and away from you to make the second loop. This loop should be about the same size as the first one. As you continue to form the loops, hold the center of the bow with your holding hand.

❺ Repeat the process of twisting and looping the ribbon so that the "right" side shows on the outside. Alternate loops below and above your holding hand until you have 5 or 6 loops on each side. All loops should be about the same size. Again, the short tail you started off with should be at the center of your bow and you should end on the opposite side. Trim off the excess ribbon.

❻ Secure the bow by tying a piece of curling ribbon, chenille stem, or florist wire around the center. Tie or twist off in the back of the bow. Leave the ends long enough to tie around your lei.

❼ Pull the loops into place to shape the bow.

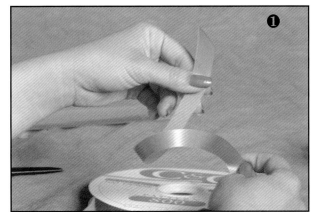

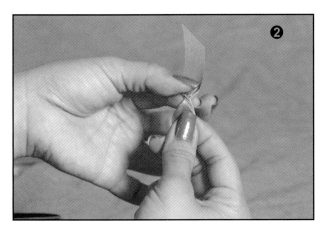

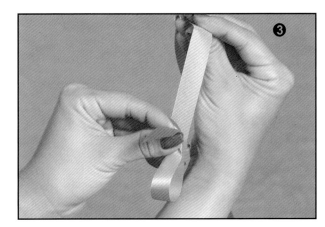

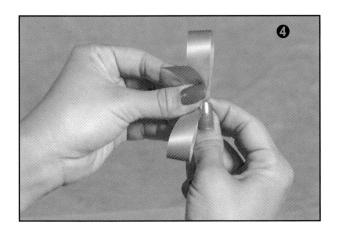

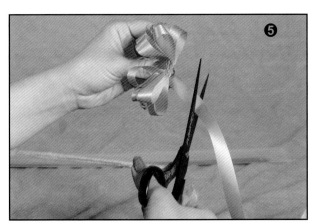

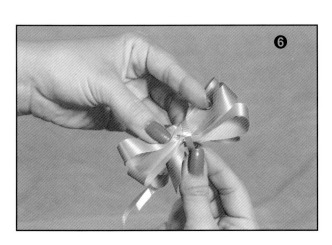

Money Rose

- 3 to 5 crisp, clean bills of any denomination
- 1 pkg. #30-gauge wire
- 1 pkg. #18-gauge wire
- 1 pkg. 1 $3/4$-in. x $5/8$-in. poly calyx
- 1 roll $1/2$-in. florist tape
- 3 to 6 seed stamen (plain or pearlized)
- wire cutters
- scissors

Creating the petals

❶ Fold one bill in half, with the portrait in the centerfold. Open the bill so that the portrait side is facing up.

❷ Curl all four corners of the bill outward. Get the curl started and then use your fingers to "rock and roll" the corners into tight curls.

❸ Find the centerfold line and pinch toward the center from the edges, gathering the bill on the line.

❹ Bend one-half of a #30-gauge wire in half. Place the bend over the portrait side of the center of the bill and twist tie at the back as tightly as possible. This will form two petals. Push into the center area of each petal, to create the cupped effect.

Adding more petals

Repeat steps 1–4 until you have the desired number of petal sets. Use no more than five sets per flower.

Putting it all together

❺ Place three to six stamens in the middle of one set of petals. This will be the center of your flower, so choose a set that is more "closed" than the others. Do not twist the wires together.

❻ Place the next set of petals so that it sits in the opposite direction of the first set. Place another set of petals so that it sits in the same direction as the first set. Place the last two sets on each side of the flower so that the petals fill in the empty spaces.

❼ Push the wires of the rose through the hole in the center of the calyx. The cupped shape of the calyx will help to keep the shape of the rose.

❽ For the stem, poke a #18-gauge wire up through the bottom of the calyx. Secure with florist tape. Add rose leaves and secure with florist tape.

Tips:
• Do not twist the wires of the petals and stamen. The wires need to be straight and as slim as possible to fit into the hole of the calyx.
• For a realistic-looking rose, when you attach the leaves to the stem, leave some space at the top under the flower head. (A real rose never has leaves growing up against the head of the flower.) Also, stagger the leaves so that they are not evenly placed.

Fairy

- 1 each silk flower, French tulip
- 1 each wooden doll head, natural
- 2 bundles cloth forget-me-not flowers, assorted colors
- 4 yards $^3/_8$-in. metallic polyester ribbon, gold or silver

1 yd. #40 wired chiffon ribbon, white/gold
- 1 each whispering grass (or princess pine)
- 1 roll $^1/_2$-in. florist tape
- 1 each #30-gauge florist wire
- 1 each chenille stem, white
- 1 each tinsel chenille stem, gold
- Spanish moss
- acrylic paints, black and white
- 1 each BBQ stick   • blush   • hot glue gun   • scissors

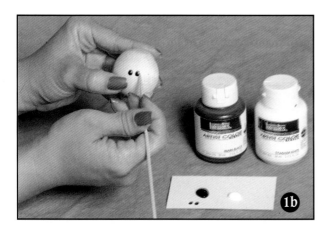

❶ Prepare the doll head first so that the paint will dry by the time you are ready to mount it.

a. Using the BBQ stick, dip the flat end into black paint and "stamp" two dots for the doll's eyes on the wooden head. (You may want to practice making dots of the same size on a piece of paper first.)

b. Next, dip the sharp end of the BBQ stick into some white paint and add a tiny dot on each eye. You'll be surprised how this little detail really makes the eyes "shine."

c. Set the head aside to allow the paint to dry.

❷ Prepare the fairy's dress.

a. Choose a flower with a head large enough to create the fairy's dress. Find one that has a stamen in the center. This will help secure it to the stem in step 2d.

b. Cut the flower head from the stem, leaving about $^1/_4$" of the stem at the base.

c. Remove any leaves or thorns from the flower stem.

d. Open up the petals of the flower. Carefully squeeze some hot glue onto the top end of the stem.

e. Attach it to the center of the flower. If the flower has a stamen, use florist tape to secure it to the stem.

f. Then cover the entire length of the stem with florist tape.

g. Starting at the top, wrap the entire stem with the gold or silver ribbon. Wrap in small sections and apply hot glue to each section.

❸ Attach the head to the dress.

a. Use your fingertip (or a cotton swab) to add some blush to the doll's cheeks.

b. Insert the base of the flower into the doll head. You may have to trim the stem so the head will sit flush to the flower.

c. Remove the head and squeeze some hot glue into the well.

d. Close the petals of the flower and insert the base of the flower into the glue, attaching the doll head.

e. Allow the glue to cool and bond.

❹ Give her some arms to hold a gift or a special wish.

a. Bend the tinsel chenille stem in half, to mark the center. Hot glue the center of the chenille stem to the back of the doll's head at the base, just where it meets the dress. Allow the glue to cool and bond.

b. Hook the arms together at the desired length (consider what you will want her to hold in her hands) and trim the excess with a wire cutter.

❺ Give her some wings to fly.

a. Overlap the ends of a 9- to 10-in. piece of #40 wired chiffon ribbon, forming a circle. Secure scantly with hot glue. Flatten the circle, keeping the overlapped area in the center.

b. Pinch the outer edges of the ribbon together at the center and twist a piece of white chenille stem around the center to secure the ribbon, forming her wings.

c. Hot glue the wings to her back, hiding the tinsel chenille at the base of the head.

❻ She deserves a lovely head of hair and a haku.

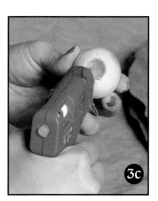

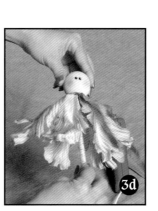

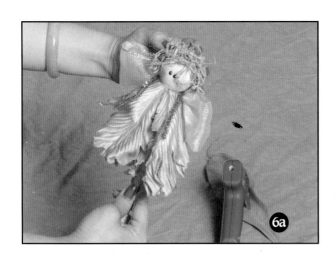

a. Carefully hot glue some Spanish moss to her head to create her hair. You may want to gather a little at a time before gluing it to her head.

b. Hot glue a piece of whispering grass (or princess pine) to her head. Start with the center in line with her face and work your way to the back on each side. The two ends should meet in the back.

c. Glue some flowers to the greenery to give her a *haku* head *lei*.

Special touches:

• Add a bow with some streamers to give her a festive look.
• For graduation, have her hold a folded monetary fan or rose or a small bag with a little gift inside (i.e., jewelry or the key to a new car).

1 in.

7/8 in.

2 1/4 in.

1 3/4 in.

1 1/4 in.

2 in.

43

Marking Grid

Marking Grid 44~

1/2 in.

2 1/2 in.

5/16 in.

1 1/2 in.

1/4 in.